And If I Go With Child?

Reimagining
The Mysteries
of Tam Lin

Charlotte Hussey

And If I Go With Child?

Reimagining
The Mysteries
of Tam Lin

Charlotte Hussey

ISBN: 978-99987-719-3-2 (perfectbound)
ISBN: 978-99987-719-4-9 (epub)

Published 1 February, 2024 by
RITONA
3 rue de Wormeldange
Rodenbourg, L-6955
LUXEMBOURG

Editing and Design by RITONA

For more information about our works:
distro@abeautifulresistance.com
abeautifulresistance.org

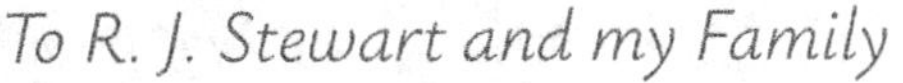

To R. J. Stewart and my Family

Within

Introduction

An immersion into the medieval ballad of "Tam Lin" will reveal "the secrets of initiation in the Faery tradition," claims R.J. Stewart, an authority on Celtic mythology and Faery (*Well* 152). Reading this, I was intrigued. I teach medieval literature and particularly Breton faery lais. I decided to test his claim by using my own poetry to explore the Scottish, supernatural ballad, "Tam Lin." Stewart goes on to say that meditation on such a ballad can bring "our own imaginations alive" through its archetypal characters and symbols (*Underworld* 171). Janet, the ballad's feisty heroine, quickly stirred me to adapt her persona in many of my poems. Inspired by Janet's strong will and powerful love magic, I began piecing together a young woman's coming of age story, a portrait of her sensual, sexual, and imaginative awakening. Her adventures, although situated in the Scottish Lowlands during the middle ages, resonate in many ways with my own.

Francis James Child classified "Tam Lin" as a narrative ballad. "Tam Lin" tells a story of captivity and liberation by way of redemptive love. I have adhered to this plotline. But because the traditional ballad also moves easily between voices, time periods, and worlds, I have relied less on causal relationships and more on acausal, meaning-related ones. Using the ballad's lines as prompts, I went on a search for evocative images from any time period, or place that spoke to these lines. I built collages with them for sections of "Tam Lin." I then free-wrote about the collaged images and pulled out energized passages to form poem skeletons. I built up and cut back numerous times, winnowing my words into these poems. This a-causal structure has also allow the magical and supernatural to more easily break through.

I have prefaced each section of this book with the corresponding "Tam Lin" ballad stanzas, so you can read, in its entirety, one of Child's version (there are many). I will also provide a quick synopsis of the "Tam Lin" narrative to prevent you from being pixy-lead into a bog: A Scottish king forbids the maidens in his court to visit Carterhaugh Woods because they will have to pay a fee (their virginity) to its spectral guardian, Tam Lin. The king's daughter immediately runs to the woods and is impregnated by Tam Lin. She tries to abort their baby until she finds out her faery knight is really a human in thrall to the Faery Queen. Janet must rescue Tam Lin on Halloween. If she fails to do so, the Queen will sacrifice her captive to pay a tithe to hell.

The question remains: has this my immersion into the medieval ballad, "Tam Lin," initiated me into Faery. I will leave that to you, dear reader, to decide.

The Ballad of Tam Lin

The King forbad his maidens a'
that wore gold in their hair,
tae come or go by Carterhaugh
for the young Tam Lin is there.

And those that go by Carterhaugh
from them he tak's a fee
either their rings or their mantles,
or else their maidenheed.

So Janet has kilted her green mantle
just a little above her knee,
and she has gane tae Carterhaugh
just as fast as she cud flee.

Carterhuagh, There Not There

I will sing you an old
ballad that opens a footpath,
scented by doe and fawn.
Swaths of bending grasses
and berry bushes hide
its worn way into a wood,
a wood that always waits
for us, sating itself
on leaf-mold and runoff.

Its path meanders up
rocky outcrops and down
through a maze of black maple,
red spruce, and pine.
A jay whistles a warning.
A warbler's watery voice
calls me to the brook.

> I watch long-legged
> water striders skate
> over the tea-brown waves.
> Perched on tawny reeds,
> roused frogs utter
> throaty twangs and plash,
> stroking webbed feet
> like oars. A branch floats
> towards shore. A boat!

They debark on a foot-sized
beach. Dewy forms.
Spider webs from the arching
ferns they pass under
lace their frocked coats
and silver-green gowns.

I piece together their huts
from sticks strewn by eddies
up the bank and fistfuls
of grass, cutting my hands
worse than school paper.

A bush shakes a man out of it.
He's stubby as a rough root.
His face is overgrown with hair
and shadows. His back bends
under bundle tied with a vine.

His words, a guttural rush
of water over stone. Its undertone
snags limbs, sinks leaves.
It sends goosebumps down
my arms, clouds my sight.
My village stands empty.

The bush trembles. He's
vanished, leaving behind
a lingering smell of piney
pitch and wood smoke.
At my feet, his bundle
tied with a woody vine.

I will sing you an old ballad
that opens a path deep
into a wood. The wood always
waits for us. Will you
join me?

Evening Primrose

The scrape of Father's ornate
chair legs draw closer.
The black iron mantel clock
strikes past curfew — "No! No!"
"You're wearing the evidence!" he rasps —
surprising himself — through his nose,
cawing from his high branch.

Yellow petals crown my head
with their sweet, sharp scent.
I am forbidden to answer back.
I spill over the Persian rug
a thin shadow whose stealth
slips me through keyholes
with thieving faeries to pluck
what blooms in the night.

Harvest

1. Sweet Grass

In the August heat, puffs of fog
skim the marsh like white birds.
Though kept in the yard by Father,
I know the South Wind lies
down with the North, hidden
in the reeds from prying eyes. I
look: dandelion fluff floats
over the spiked fence poles,
over the beach road, its potholes
filled with sea and and shells.
A battered blue Ford's pulled
in beside the ditch. Its windows
opened to the salt air told
its family what marsh this is.
Armed with sickles, they bend
to their work, caps pulled down
boots planted. Blades strike
cattail stock from root.
Others on their knees, gather
sweet grass. Small cuts on
thumbs and fingers leave
trickles of blood for the marsh gods.

2. Marsh Rose

It's not the sweet grass I'm here for,
although I know by its scent.
It threads this damp hillock
where mice, after the garden, circle
shiny ribbons into nests, grasses
that lace together a deceptive carpet
boots wade and sink across.

I didn't come in the blue Ford
parked by the road's boggy edge.
I follow the flute-like bubbling
of a lark, the churr of crickets,
hopping and trailing a brown syrup
to where a bush roots in black
mud, blooms with marsh roses.

     Only the girl behind the gate sees me.
I mutter old words over a cupped rose.
Yellow puffs of pollen waft up,
idling and drifting. Who am I,

a lingering loamy scent,
a shadow the bush casts off,
capped in tendrils and thorns?

Circa 1964

Wobbling my head slightly
like the earth on its axis, I tilt
birdlike, about to fledge from under
teased hair, feathered bangs.
I've been turned sunny side by
the photographer for the yearbook shoot.
Pearls drop from my ears
on silvery cords, as I fancy
the camera's click. Will he
notice? My plucked eyebrows,
accent notes still unsung,
and forbidden lipstick? So what!
The photo's a black and white.

How I make myself up.
Licked to a shine, tasting
of Revlon Wine, lips
force a smile considering
the future. My starched, white
secretarial blouse with its
tight neck to rise through,
industrious, obedient,
not meant for much, no
words except those taken
by short hand. "And please
no lipstick on the job."

No Second Thoughts

I run over the moor,
green, borders uncertain,
glide through boggy patches,
thighs awash in mist.

Head thrown back,
mouth open, I meet
the light-footed breeze,
scented with far-off

pastures, the summer sea.
It flutters my lacy collar
just above my heart
like fingers, tapping

spells I can't resist.
I pass prickly burdock
and blackberry bushes
decked in spider webs.

They catch a gust and fill
like sails on a fair sea.
My giddy sleeves swell.
Tiers of red chiffon

float off my shoulders.
My blouse flaps. The fresh
wind brushes my waist.
I'm touched everywhere.

Nipped by berry canes,
shoes caked in mud,
I soar over the soggy,
wellaway earth. I go
where the wind goes.
Only the wind knows.

And when she come tae Carterhaugh
Tam Lin was at the well,
that is his horse was there
but awa' was himsel.

She hadnae pu'ed a double rose
a rose but three or fair
when up and spoke the young Tam Lin
cried, "Lady pu'nae mair!"

"How dare ye pu' those flo'ors,
how dare ye break those wands,
how dare ye cam tae Carterhaugh
withouten my command?"

She says, "Caterhaugh it is my ain
my daddy gave it t'me,
and I will cam and gae by here
withouten any leave of thee!"

Mare at the Well

She waits, up to her hocks
in greenery. The white mare
waits. Where is her rider?
Just the sun curries her sides.

She knows the old well
for what it is, a pool
where marsh thistles and wild
roses quench their thirst.

She drinks. A pipe jets
her refreshment into the pool
from rubbly caverns where the old
powers still wander.

What can the well say
about the rider? Does he
hear without ears,
see without eyes,
like ripples of water breaking
against stone?

The Fool on the Hill

Wheels braked on the cliff's edge,
he perches on the roof of his rusty van,
pulled there from the hairpin turns
of his dreams by the promise of dawn.
His butt cheeks rest on a rug, itchy
with wizened grass from a love-in,
or some Winnebago campground
where he seeks his father's ghost.

Back east, he slammed shut
the Great Books and dodged
the draft agent's commands.
His barely zit-free chin bristles
with a don't-tread-on-me beard.
My mannish boy! A green sweatshirt
rumples under his armpits.
Thrift store jeans, their twill
wrinkle like the *arroyos* he's passed,
as the road map emptied itself of
its ghost towns and route numbers.

The dawn is reviving too much of him.
Volts shoot out. Amid thorns,
a sparrow tings, trills. Eyes
stare, sucked like eggs from their shells
by a snake side-winding through his drug-laced
mind. Scales glitter in riverbed debris:
sculls, horns, scattered bones
the sun skinned and left to be polished
by blowing sand. All night,
the abysmal god of the crossroads

pelted him with sharp stones,
until he was detritus, prima matter,
a worried grain in a desert
of grains the wind owns.

Loitering on the roof of his van,
he clutches at a crumpled letter.
Its drift, fluttered by the dry breeze,
he can't catch. Drops of blue ink
from me, his faraway girl who studies
the arabesques of an Asian alphabet,
or from his mother where sorrow finds her,
seep across its pages, distilled
from a ragged, overtaking cloud.

As the wind plays with his mind,
he climbs with a hawk, black wings
puffed up like shoulder pads
for football or for war. He screams,
eyes round as the world.

His big man boots, their fat
yellow laces, dangle untied,
far off the ground. The radio
sings of the fool on the hill,
"well on his way, head in a cloud,"
as sun catching mica chips
strewn along the lift-off ledge
flash their warnings. Pebbles
riled by the wind's insistent hiss,
ping and ricochet down, down,
no ground to call their own.

Taken

I reach into bristling
green canes, their red
ripening hips to pick
a wild, double rose.

Ouch! I gash my finger
on a stiff, grey thorn.
Hot sun on my head.
Blowsy blooms loosen

their perfumes over me.
The rose bush holds
sway, or something does.
Musk scent. Purple

stocks rise from its skullcap.
Toothed leaves bite
at my lips. Fleshy petals
brush chin, throat,

my breasts. Seeds, slightly
hairy spill. I gather
my torn, blood-spotted
skirts over my scratched
thighs. Disbelief!

Beastie

I happen upon a boundary
stone. At its base, lizards
sun, drink in the heat.
A black adder glides
its rippling shadow into patch
of nodding bluebells.

On this block of stone,
a boldly incised snake sidewinds;
its jagged strike of lightning
explodes with seeds,
budding flowers.

Just below, carved fins
clasp the rock's red granite
like those of an exhausted swimmer
clinging to a reef. Dolphin
calf or welp of a dragon,
it turns a sea-bleached snout
over a briny shoulder.

I'm suddenly sleepy.
My body knows.

Annunciation Dream

Oh to dream of standing
on a blue-green globe, wearing
a crown of 12 stars. The corner
of my blue cape would ripple
over a new moon, cycling
beneath my feet. I'd supplicate
a white dove, my virginal face
turned upwards, my meek hands
crossed over my heart.

I crouch, a naked Eve.
My breasts, brown nipples
spill into the sandy foreground
of a hidden inlet. The tide's
flat out. The moon full.

I have no beach towel
to beat at the air. I round
my red mouth, red
as first blood, and scream
at the awful humming of wings.
Knocked to my knees, pressed
wide open from behind,
I dig my toes into what
was unblemished sand.

Pulled to his plumy chest,
I'm a blade of beach grass,
bent by a hard squall.
His tongue twists, flames,

burns the near air,
spews his amorous news.

Airy drops rain down
wetting nothing, tinted
blue by the night sky, by
my tears. No emotion troubles
the yellow pupils of his eyes.
Three beams of light from each
leave hypnotic traces on the air,
heavy with his odor, part church
incense, part waxy quills.

His boneless fingers bend
to conjure newborn shapes
from perturbed clouds of matter,
a slippery, pink brood they fall
all around, or from me?
I wake, hands crossed
over my heart.

There were four and twenty ladies gay
all sitting doon at chess,
and in an' cam the fairy young Janet
as green as any glass.

Up an' spake her faither dear.
He spake up meek an' mild.
"Oh alas Janet," he cried,
"I fear you go with child."

"And if I go with child
indeed it is myself tae blame.
There's not a laird in a' your hall
sall give my child his name!

Four and Twenty Ladies Gay

all sitting down at chess. They laugh
and bicker over warring queens.
I want to slip by unnoticed.
Their onyx eyes roll towards me,
taking in my queasy, green face.
They quickly stretch their board
into a forgotten flatness, the first
floor I remember, sunken
into a hill of sand, the basement
floor of our cottage where I crawl,
palms sweaty with summer heat.

A baby, my fat knees squeak
over the black and white tiles,
awkward as a garden bug,
flown by mistake into their
checkered designs. Their haughty laughter
echoes overhead. My hands reach
into the blackness of the next square.
I want to vanish there.

And If I Go With Child?

I should be taking the fish head,
nested in its brittle bones, from
dinner table to kitchen. Its eye
staring up from the greasy platter
is the green of dirty dish water,
of a drain upchucking all it has swallowed.
There everything smells of oily, fried
fish skin. I should follow the women,
through a swinging pantry door,
paprika-dusted plates of half-
eaten eggs and orphaned peas,
clinking along my arms. My pale,
green face stares from the buffet
sideboard's mirror. I fall
from grace into a hard chair.
Bitter saliva fills my mouth.
I stare at the oriental rug.
Its twining vines and sprays
of ripening cypress buds
teem and swirl around me.

Mille-Fleurs 1967

A young woman overthrown, laid
supine along the bottom of this tapestry,
you capture my eye, pulling it

down to follow your arm, stretched
out over the densely spun grass,
arms sheathed in gold baldachin

that relaxed too soon. Beside you,
a slender stock bears two lilies
stitched in creamy silk and four tightly

worked green buds, stalk
snapped by your fall into this dark field
studded with a thousand flowers.

Floating up from the primal backdrop,
flowers! Fleeting flowers: cowslips,
daisies, daffodils, forget-me-nots,

and a hare sheltered by marsh marigolds.
Higher in the leafy arabesques, a pair
of doves sing from the Book of Nature.

Modestly draped in a fine linen
couvre-chef, your head turns away
from their drawn-out, nesting calls

to show me the pains some weaver
took to touch with her pale threads
your downturned lips, blanched

cheeks, eyes rolled back.
Three fatal sisters, towering boldly
above you, are also weaving.

Clotho, the youngest fate, secures
her distaff in the golden chains of her girdle,
raising it like a royal scepter, wrapped

with gossamer flax fine as a girl's hair.
She playfully tugs at her older sister,
tugs at Lachesis' samite gown,

laughing at the thought of us weaving
a cloth imperial, its threads wrapped
in Hephaestion copper, silver, and gold.

Lachesis' sliding fingers, rhythmically
pull flax from the distaff, twisting,
wetting it with her supernatural spittle.

She methodically measures you
hardly a yard of played thread,
presses her foot into your rib cage,

as if to push out your last breath,
like a lady adept at *l'art de venerie,*
preparing to cut the throat of her prey.

Atropos, the eldest fate, poses
as a nun with a rosary of corals and crystal,

her sleeves trimmed in Siberian sable.

No spindle rests against her black
serge thigh to twirl and stretch
your stiffening thread. Empty hand,

her long liturgical fingers spill
a last blessing like an early frost
over your fallen head, dropped

without warning as I was dropped

on a hospital gurney and wheeled
into a brick-walled, back room
by a frosty, blue-bearded doctor.

Clad in crisp, surgical scrubs,
armored with his breastplate of vows
to protect the sick, the weak, the innocent,

he said, "If you are deflowered, pregnant,
I'll let you die." Cyst. Rupture. Pain.
Like you I turned my head away,

alone in a flowerless cell, minus
your droll monkey and attendant hare.
I lay on a cot in a tiny room,

watching the sun through a small window
rise outside on a bleak wall.
Tomb by tomb. It climbed,

flushing the bricks a fiery red.

And Janet has kilted her green mantle
just a little above her knee,
and she has gain tae Carterhaugh
for tae pu' the scathing tree.

"How dare ye pu' those flo'ors
all amang the leaves sae green,
an'ye wud kill that bonnie babe
that we gat us between."

She says,"Ye must tell tae me Tam Lin,
ah ye must tell tae me
were ye e'er a mortal knight,
or mortal hall did see?"

Willow

Strewn with deadfall,
the path thins, snagged
by a break of jack pines;
I plunge through nettles,
ferns, boggy wallows,
burs sticking to the socks
I've pulled over my jeans.

Pushed aside branches,
red-tipped ones, snap
back, whipping my cheeks,
as my tearing eyes blur.
Shaggy brown bark,
mist-filled knotholes,
a narrow face peers out.

A summer shawl of long,
lance-shaped leaves cascades
over her shoulder. A willow
maiden leans from her tree.
My eyes clear. A doe
with silver, leaf-shaped ears,
is leaping away.

My fingers trace the blow
left by her hoof, a two-toed
print, a shattered heart.

Picking Penny Royal

1.

I kneel in a loamy ditch
where forest meets field,
sheltering under a pine
on this cool June day.
Tiny blossoms, their bending
stems creep around me.

Light plays across a mossy
clod of earth. It arrives
to dapple the plump knuckle
of my baby finger before
it curls into shadow.

I drop my heart unseen
into the hollow of my chest,
into the peppermint scent of coarse
leaves, their purple florets,
their pin-cushion blooms.

My hands tremble to pluck
medicine from this sprawling web.
My knees press the mud
where others have, a stunning scullery
maid toyed with by her lord,

a Roma girl raped on a country lane,
even a smitten queen.

Someone has driven a branch
into the sod. It rises up
leafless and straight beside me.
A memorial? A sign? "Pick
here. Pick what you must!"

2.

I rest on the grassy bank,
pretending I'm a fine lady
featured in a medieval herbal
dressed in a chartreuse robe.
I recline on an immaculate cot,
draped in bleached muslin,
awaiting the goblet of warm wine.

In my reverie an herbalist
looms beside me in this glade,
her gown dark as the spills
of the nearby hemlock. She
cradles a sprig of penny royal
against her shoulder. Looking
sternly down at the red
mortar and pestle, she is grinding
grey green leaves to bits.
The grating grows more rhythmic,
scrape, scrape of pestle,
against the blood red bowl.

3.

A small cloud of midges
works at their slender
legged mating dance.
I scooch below them
in my ditch, entangled
in a dense, green mat
of leafy stems and flowers.
I sit groggy, hungry.

Fog like a cry rises
from the ground. Its damp
tendrils swathe a figure.
It faces me behind a thinning,
hazy wall. A fist
pushes defiantly through
a billowing sleeve of mist
to strike a blow? Tam Lin?

The swam of midges reels,
their winged rondeau of spins
and dives buzzes closer.
From their lowland bacchanal,
biting words fly:
"How dare you kill our babe?"

I was onc't a mortal knight,
I cam riding here one day,
and I fell fram aff my horse.
The Faery Queen stole me awa."

"Tomorrow night is Hallowe'en,
and the faery folk do ride.
Those that wud their true love win
at Miles Cross they must hide."

"First ye let pass the black horse
then ye let pass the broun,
run ap tae the milk white steed
and pu' the rider doon."

"I Tam a Lin on a milk white steed
wi' a gold star in my croon.
Because I was a mortal knight,
they give me such reknown."

How the Faery Queen Stole Tam Lin

"Sleep thou, and I will wind thee in my arms....
so doth the woodbine, the sweet honeysuckle,
gently entwist."
Shakespeare, *Midsummer Night's Dream*

1

Out hunting and thirsty,
he and his horse happen
upon an abandoned well.
Black thorns guard it.
The mare stumbles, the boggy
ground gives way. Brown eyes
bulge, roll back. Nostrils flare
in her big boned head. What
spooks her, a mouse scurrying
under a rose shrub, a hissing
pipe, a water sucking drain?

She jumps sideways, rears.
Her hooves pummel the air.
The reins rip from his hands.
Knees can't grip her flanks.
Whipped off the swaying
saddle, he falls. His brain rolls
into the dark, a muddy pebble
sinking deeper. The water trills,
its tinkly, piercing notes
no horse can prance to.

2

A grasshopper roosts
on a stout blade of grass,
swaying its feelers over
its bulbous, meadow green
all-seeing eyes: the pair
wave as if to wake visions,
making the large small,
the small grow large.

A regal woman parts
the ferns, their tips, pointed
spears, tower over her.
Beetle on the ribbed shaft
of a reedy pillar, a tuft
at its top, probes and climbs,
its black armor polished
with heavy, sweet dew.

Crowned in golden
honeysuckle blossoms,
their twining stems bejeweled
with blood red berries,
she's almost beautiful,

small lips a bit tight,
tiny nostrils like dark
pinholes against the white,
white side of her face,
the other side, shadowy.

She's not moved by how
his perfectly wrenched back
twists beneath his green tunic
and into the trampled grass.

Snort of the horse that threw him.
Chirp of a grasshopper rubbing
spurred leg to wing.

Midnight, Miles' Crossing

"On the run."
ExxonMobil

Red Pegasus has faded
and fled this Mobil gas
station, leaving his winged
trace on a worn sign.
Twin pumps go on
guarding their lonely island,
where slack rubber hoses
hang useless as a bridle
not buckled up in time.

I'm called to pull in
and take the fresh air
before driving the steep, dirt
road home. I'm called
by steel strings twanging
from the locked-up garage.

A country voice croons
from the ol' brown radio
stationed on a dusty side-shelf.
Miles, closing his cash,
probably forgot to spin
its gold dial to off.

The voice, stark, mournful,
plays riveting tricks,
sliding Jonny Cash over
the harmonizing airwaves

to the granite stoop. He sets
his lumbering body down.

Clad in a long black
coat, preacher or gunslinger,
he cradles his guitar like a lover
brought back from the dead.
He warms his chilled fingers,
takes spooky baseline
walks down the frets.

Just a wayfaring stranger
soon to slip unnoticed
into the rat-gnawed shed
for some hobo sleep, he strums
to the hiss and clatter of a train
chugga-loo, chugga-lugging
past the Baptist graveyard,
past the owl in the piney wood.

He starts to sway, seized
by a rough and tumble rapture.
His gravelly drawl troubles
the midnight air, as if
a roving haunt rises up
from under the tarmac
and growls its secret pain
through him. Its roughshod
rumble works to uncross
the roads for ghost riders.

Specks at first surge
out of exile from back

of the West Wind. Their hurling
mass sucks fire from the stars
they pass, whooping, riding
hard across the fenceless,
Great Plains of the Sky.

Gutted pumpkins sputter
and glare. Dogs howl.
A whip of lightning strikes
a skeletal sapling. Green
bark cracks, smoking
by the oily culvert, ashes
all that remains of a hobo's fire.

Heart of Stone

Who nests a black, heart-
shaped stone on a pile
of white branches?
What hands stack up
these limbs, bleached
by the sun, their bark
flayed? What words
whispered over the stone's
edges, chaffed, chipped
by rasp and hammer? Who lights
the dry twigs crackling
into flames fed by winds,
flames withering the roost
to ash, as the white-hot stone
sinks into the tended pit,
its smoky juices oozing
anger, frustration, and joy?

Faery Riders at Miles' Gas Station

A summoned cloud, we
riders are condensing into a faceless
troupe. We wait. Our Queen,
will she say us into trees,
an overflowing river, a flock of sparrows?
Better said, our horses
stand square. Ears
prick forward for her commands.
Mine snorts, paws
at the paved-over earth,
to test the sheer span
of what is and what is not.

We escort the human on the white horse.
Tam Lin she calls him, the one
she has fattened with honey cakes
and rose hip wine.
He is to be sacrificed to pay
our Queen's tithe to Hell.

We trot past a strange building.
She scoffs, points to what
she calls their Time Keeper;
he peers out at us
from behind a glass pane.
His beardless, round face
is blemished by black dagger
blades for arms or hands
and a dashing red needle
orbiting like a meteor's tail.

In his lackluster courtyard,
a leafless, long-stemmed plant
towers, topped by its unreachable
saucer-shaped flower,
or is it a dying moon, shackled
like war booty to a pole?
It sheds a flickering, anemic
light over this north-facing
shrine, over its two pillars,
rising from a pitted altar-slab.
Metallic, round-headed
cousins of their crippled god,
each pillar seems clad in a butcher's
apron, soiled red.

Nothing glows here
with the high polish of our gold.
Dull bits of pewter
cap hooked and dangling,
rubbery snakes—to be boiled
in an oily-smelling, propitiatory
broth? Umbilical cords?
Intestines? A tin bucket
with a bird's beak—fetish
of an avenging vulture cult?
is there, no doubt,
to catch the blood of sacrifice.

Our ways are more genteel.
When the white horse
smells fresh water,
he will thunder into the lake
and swiftly drown his rider.

Let Pass the Black and Then the Brown, Run up to the Milk White Steed and Pull Its Rider Down

Black

Black as the sun's shadow,
the mare's legs, feathery
fetlocks plunge into the grass
stained with moony tears.

I've seen her in my dreams,
as a horse-headed queen
surveying her lands from a high-
backed throne, bitter

salt piled by her side.
Briny crystals, pinched,
crushed, crumbled, whet
the hunger of lips and tongue.

The black mare's been shed
like a stone from Above,
a meteorite bathed in cloudy light.
Bones bare the impact.

Her onyx hooves reflect
the secrets of nature,
their thorny proverbs,
their flowery potions.

Brown

Rising its springy legs,
a brown yearling canters,
airborne mid-stride, pumping
energies up from Below.

Thick forelocks ripple
over the blazed forehead,
wide-set eyes,
sky blue flames,

and delicate muzzle. The brown
blows through big teeth
and darts like inspiration or water
over a mirror. Colt or filly?

Can't tell from here.
A horse head's a rebis
alchemists say you can fashion
into anything you want:

Christ, drops of blood
fall from his gashed side,
mana fertilizing belief,
outside the city gates
on a skull-shaped hill,

or a she-dragon. Fiery
cinnabar oozes from her beak.
Vermillion tongue lashes,
spews a poisonous slaver
that is stirring the grasses to life.

Message-bringer, misunderstood
prophet, the brown nickers
to the listening grasses: The One
is Two, the Two One.

White

His sweating sides flash
like lightning from the high-piled
clouds. His molten mane

melts over his lofty neck
marked with whorls of hair
the Roma say bring luck.

Contained by his creamy pelt,
he is vast inside and out,
as he floats over green earth.

His unreadable eyes,
disintegrate into the rippling dots
of an expanding universe,

he is a white heat, a being
of pure will, ferocious,
impossible to take alive.

Do I see a shape
coalesce in the heated vapors,
astride his smoky back,

a rider condensing as if
in an alembic, unkempt,
sun-struck, dazed?

Tail fanning fire behind him,
the stallion trails a brimstone scent.
All the shadows of the earth

rise up, caught in his sulphury
wake, awakener of death.

Rescue

A hoar frost rims
the wrinkled leaves of golden rod,
the blackthorns' prickly spears.
I hide in a wind-stirred,
scrubby patch of cover,
waiting for the crossroads to open.
Where I kneel, the brittle grasses
revive, sweet and green.
Summer surrounds me.

I unpin my brooch, let
fall my cape. My breasts
bare, soft against
my belly, I lean them
close over the earth,
call upon its green
force to quicken my heart.

The Faery Queen, enveloped
in her ice blue gown,
beaded with frost spikes
and blinding crystal shards,
can blast me dumb,
or dead with her blighting breath.
She trots up with her riders.

Bridles ring. Tam Lin
wears a starry crown.
He sits rigid in the saddle.
His gaze blank. His horse

hesitates, peering down
at the rocks, the jutting roots.
Tam Lin lurches, sways.

I grab his leather boot,
pull him from his death-
ride on the white horse,
the one overstepping, parading
close to the human world,
the one lured by my love
like sugar in the hand.

"First they'll change me in your airms
intae some snake or adder.
Hold me close and fear me not
for I'm yair child's fadder."

"Next they'll change me in your airms
intae a lion wild.
Hold me close and fear me not
just as yu'ld hold your child."

"Then they'll change me in your airms
into a burning gleed.
Throw me into well water
and throw me in with speed."

"Last they'll change me in your airms
into a mother-naked knight.
Wrap me up in your green mantle,
and hide me close from sight."

So weel she did what he did say
she did her tru'love win
and wrapt him up in her mantle
as blithe any bird in Spring.

Hold Me Tight

1. Snake

Hold tight like the pet
store girl. Her jagged
black hair's streaked
a blood red, as if a fire
seethes from her scalp.
A choker collars her neck,
studded with faux-rubies
stolen from a dragon's hoard.

Her arms are swathed in glam
black warmers, stitched
with seven fiery Wonder
Woman stars, a sexy
safeguard against what
she holds : a grey body
with black saddle markings
all along his rat-fed,
upward easing length.
His forked tongue
flicks a near kiss.

He scales her like a tree,
gliding his smooth skin
over her pelvis, her waist,
a maenad's overcome
by his surging weight.

Behind her are tanks for toads
of a baleful breath, scorching

basilisks, and blood lusting
fish. Jurassic fronds
uncoil their plumes. Ashen
sand flanks steamy
baths lit by bulbs,
warming the coldest blood.

Her Cleopatra eyes,
wing-tailed with black kohl
stare entranced, as she
grips his thick shuddering
girth. His tail lashes.
She staggers.

A marijuana pendant
sways its prosperous green
leaves over her heart,
a bobble he is sizing up.
He's poised, rows of hooked
teeth primed to latch,
hold on tight.

2. Lion

Hold tight like the odalisque,
or naughty circus girl.
A spotlight high up
in the cosmic rigging beams
its silvery rays down.
Roan hair, bare
breasts with rhinestone pasties.

Her navel flashes its ruby.

Loins barely concealed
by the filmy, see-through
folds of a courtesan's skirt,
she strikes her charming pose:
Diana of the Wild Hunt,
goddess of the animals and the moon.

She provokes us
with an arrow, delicately poised
between thumb and forefinger,
one drawn from her snake-
embroidered belt quiver
draped over her sex.

She aims its red tip
at a gold pelted lion
like a shaman at her spirit prey.
Victoriously tender,
she embraces his terrible shape,
tilts his massive head.
His wiry solar mane
chafes her sparkling nipples.

Claws sheathed for now,
eyes narrowed to slits,
he lazes against her, indulging
in a before dinner nap.

Can she who turns men
into beasts, bring him back?

Gleed

This scalding gleed
tumbles, perturbed, meteoric,
shedding space dust
and yellow gases.

Ripples of light
ring the rim of a well,
a nimbus the hot gleed
hurls headlong through,
as if thrust by a blacksmith
into his quenching tub.

Summoned by the chime
of midnight bells, he sinks,
hissing and steaming into a deep
shaft of blue water.
Tempered, his mettle hardens.

Two Lights

Primroses bloom. Luna
tarries under a starry
vault, statuesque and naked,
her skin light yellow,
or is it translucent white?

Arrayed with her orange sickle,
her half-shaven head
trails a side-fall of light,
as she peers into a well,
searching for her lover Sol.

Blue faced, he floats up,
mouth open like a fish.
Flames flicker and stream.
His seething head burns
the well's green surface.

Tireless, Luna is reversing
time, raising him up
from his watery coffin, a king
she has bathed and made firm
for their love making.

Gingerly stepping a foot
to the ground, the other
poised on the well's rim,
Sol hesitates, an initiate
from a Netherworld ordeal.

Red-brown biceps
ripple and swell; he hugs
Luna's creamy shoulder,
burying his head there,
momentarily her devotee.

Sol and Luna, her hair's
a golden veil. His head
erupts with bold spokes.
Their embrace decks each
leaf of a little bush
rooted by the pebbled path,
their wedding guest,
with beads of light.

Green Mantle

On the first of a cool November,
he shivers, clutching his crotch.
I stand him between two pines,
wrap him in my mantle. Green

this earthly garment, worked
with leafy tendrils. Ivy
spirals, stem-stitched round
its hem. He leans into me.

eases the heaviness in his head
into the folds of its hood. He sways
woozy like one wading
through chest-deep water to shore.

Is he 21 or 990 years old
like the withered Children of Lir?
He stares at his hands, pink,
supple, or spotted and veined?

A seedpod rattles, sends
an ache rippling across
his brain. He stands perplexed,
trying to remember his name.

Up and spake the Faery Queen
from oot a bush o' broom,
"Oh alas my sisters 'a
young Tam Lin has escaped his doom.

Up and spake the Faery Queen
and angry cried she,
"If I had know of this Tam Lin
that some lady'd borrowed thee..."

"If I had known of this Tam Lin
that some lady'd borrowed thee,
I'd pluck out thine eyes of flesh
And put in eyes of a tree..."

"If I had known of this Tam Lin
before we cam frae home,
I'd plucked out thin heart of flesh
and put in a heart of stone."

The Faery Queen

1

Homesickness seizes some
in spite of how I spice
my frothy, rose-hip wine.
I pluck out their eyes,
put in those of a tree,
plugged tight with grainy
bark. They leave blind
to how we go about
stealing what we will.

My lovers fear the tumble
back into time like a tree
fallen on hard ground.
I fill damp mouths
with clumps of moss. I bind
limbs and hands with tangled
vines. I call up
squalls of snow to blanket
where they rest, given
over to my wild wood.

2

Turning my back
on this worldly romance,
I bundle the yellowing leaves
of a thorn bush around me.
I fashion my skirts into a plaid
of twisted black branches
and slender, savage briars.

Nothing flowers anymore.
I sink the way marsh
light, beyond your reach,
settles back into a bog.
Storied, spindly pines
crowd in,
knotholes everywhere.

The Sweeper

I sing as I sweep, old
ballads and new. My broom
scrapes the gas station's
rough tarmac near
opening time. I grasp
its handle of hazel wood,
sing to its steady rasp,
rasp. Its hard bristles
swirl leaves, pinecones,
drag trash scattered
by revelers into a growing pile.

Last night they screamed,
bolted down the road
to the first pumpkin-lit
porch they could find.
I clean up their taffy
wrappers, candy corn,
whiskers from a mask, a ripped
crown, a green tatter
from a fey gown.

Another masked merrymaker
visited later at night.
He knocked over the trash.
His long fingers clawed
at its choice bits—fries,
burger buns, M&Ms.
In his snug lair dug
under the shed, the raccoon

wraps his ringed tail
round himself and snores,
stomach full of sweets.

I sing to him and to you.
My broom riffs, raises
a golden dust, pushes
back the tree shadows
the waiting wood trails
over the drive. Dawn.
Customers wheeling in.

Hearts of Stone

Summer again. Janet and I
traded in our Minnie Mouse
lunchboxes for a black and gold
transistor radio. Too restless
to sit on the front porch,
the river too fast for a swim,
we rolled our short shorts
shorter and perched the radio
on one of our shoulders,
our pet black bird.
It warbled and chink-chinked
the top pop tunes, as we
walked the village roads,
looking for boys, boys
out there somewhere.

The broken sidewalk, our only
dance floor, gave way
to the gravel our sneakers scuffed
and the ditch we dove into,
saved from a hotrod. Its muffler
snorted like the bull charging
us when we crossed his field.
Its driver honked and waved.
We felt older and hot.

Our transistor radio consoled
us with song. Elvis
crooned his raw pain
just to the two of us.

All thoughts of sought
after boys vanished
into Elvis's falsetto swoops.
He hiccupped, "plea, please, please,"
pleading in a voice so contagious,
we were real gone.

We imagined him unbuttoning
a bit of his pink rockabilly
shirt, arm-wrestling
the mike, and slowing his husky
voice to grind his hips.
Our rubbery legs circled.
Our butts jiggled along
"cause they say no, no, no...
I thought I knew hearts made of stone."

We were too young to know
about hard heads and hearts
and why Elvis keened about
them. Up on stage,
he'd rise on the balls of his feet
itching to explode. Loose jointed,
unpredictable legs spread,
he'd listen for a cue from the band,
or from one of those hard-hearts
he'd met at the crossroads
where accidents happen.

Publications and Works Cited

Page 7. R.J. Stewart. *The Underworld Initiation, A Journey towards Psychic Transformation*, Lake Toxaway, Mercury Publishing, NC, 1990.

The Well of Light : From Faery Healing to Earth Healing, the Mystery of the of the Double Rose, Lake Toxaway, NC: Muse Press, 2004.

"Tam Lin" (The ballad variant used here with editing), *The Well of Light*, pp. 154-157.

Page 13. "Evening Primrose," published as "Forbid," *Montreal Serai* (Mar.21, 2013): https://montrealserai.com/article/two-new-poems/

Page 14. "Harvest" published as "Roma," *Montreal Serai* (Mar.21, 2013): https://montrealserai.com/article/two-new-poems/

Page 24. "Beastie," published as "Pictish Beastie." *The Deep Music, Offerings from the Awen*. Eds. Lorna Smithers, Greg Hill, Lia Hunter, Lulu.com, April 12, 2020: 65-66.

Page 26. "Annunciation Dream," published as "Ars Poetica," *Montreal Serai* (Dec. 26, 2013)

Page 35. *Aemilius Macer de herbarum virtutbus Apud Friburgum Brisgoicum, 1530, fol.1*: "Pellit abortuumpotu, vel subdita tantum."

Page 39. "How the Faery Queen Stole Tam Lin." *The Deep Music, Offerings from the Awen*. Eds. Lorna Smithers, Greg Hill, Lia Hunter, Lulu.com, April 12, 2020: 66-69.

Page 39. William Shakespeare, *Midsummer Night's Dream*, Act 4, Scene 1: https://myshakespeare.com/midsummer-nights-dream/act-4-scene-1

Page 42. "Midnight at Miles' Crossing," published as "Halloween, Emery's Crossing," *Eternal Haunted Summer, Winter Solstice Issue 2019*: https://eternalhauntedsummer.com/issues/winter-solstice-2019/halloween-emerys-crossing/

"On the Run (Convenience Store)," Wikipedia: https://en.wikipedia.org/wiki/On_the_Run_(convenience_store)

Page 48. "Let Pass the Black then the Brown, Run Up to the Milk White Steed and Pull its Rider Down," *Gingerbread House*, May 31, 2020: https://gingerbreadhouselitmag.com/2020/05/31/8-6/

Page 61. "Green Mantle," published as "Janet's Green Mantle." *The Deep Music, Offerings from the Awen. Eds. Lorna Smithers, Greg Hill, Lia Hunter,* Lulu.com, April 12, 2020: 69-70.

Charlotte Hussey

Growing up on a sand bar fronted by the Atlantic and backed by a tidal marsh, Charlotte Hussey writes poetry to express her love of nature and things sensuous. Teaching medieval literature at Montreal's Dawson College, she has published *Rue Sainte Famille* and *Glossing the Spoil*. Her poems can be found in *The Awen Anthology of Eco-spiritual Poetry*; *Arc Magazine*, *Antigonish Review*, *The Fiddlehead*, *Eternal Haunted Summer*, and *Gingerbread House*. She's reachable at charlotte.hussey@mcgill.

RITONA

RITONA is an imprint dedicated to publishing works of poets and mystics advocating for pluralism, tolerance, and respect for pagan, indigenous, and non-industrial ways of being in the World.

Find out more at ABEAUTIFULRESISTANCE.ORG

Printed in the USA
CPSIA information can be obtained
at www.ICGtesting.com
CBHW031232070724
11193CB00013B/625